VALEAS MUNDUM

ANDY RILEY HAS WRITTEN FOR BLACK BOOKS, TRIGGER HAPPY TV, SO GRAHAM NORTON AND SMACK THE PONY. HE HAS CO-WRITTEN THE BAFTA AWARD-WINNING ROBBIE THE REINDEER, THE RADIO FOUR PANEL GAME THE 99p CHALLENGE AND THE FORTHCOMING DISNEY ANIMATION FEATURE, GNOMEO AND JULIET. HE DRAWS ROASTED, A WEEKLY COMIC STRIP IN THE OBSERVER MAGAZINE. ANDY IS THE AUTHOR OF THE BESTSELLING THE BOOK OF BUNNY SUICIDES.

RETURN OF THE BUNNY SUICIDES

ANDY RILEY

A PLUME BOOK

PLUME

PUBLISHED BY THE PENGUIN GROUP

PENGUIN GROUP (USA) INC., 375 HUDSON STREET, NEW YORK, NEW YORK 10014, USA
PENGUIN BOOKS LTD, 80 STRAND, LONDON WC2R ORL, ENGLAND
PENGUIN BOOKS AUSTRALIA LTD, 250 CAMBERWELL ROAD, CAMBERWELL, VICTORIA 3124, AUSTRALIA
PENGUIN BOOKS CANADA LTD, 10 ALCORN AVENUE, TORONTO, ONTARIO, CANADA M4V 3B2
PENGUIN BOOKS INDIA (P) LTD, 11 COMMUNITY CENTRE, PANCHSHEEL PARK, NEW DELHI - 110 017, INDIA
PENGUIN BOOKS (NZ) LTD, CNR ROSEDALE AND AIRBORNE ROADS, ALBANY, AUCKLAND 1310, NEW ZEALAND
PENGUIN BOOKS (SOUTH AFRICA) (PTY) LTD, 24 STURDEE AVENUE, ROSEBANK, JOHANNESBURG 2196, SOUTH AFRICA

PENGUIN BOOKS LTD, REGISTERED OFFICES: 80 STRAND, LONDON WC2R ORL, ENGLAND

PUBLISHED BY PLUME, A MEMBER OF THE PENGUIN GROUP (USA) INC. THIS IS AN AUTHORIZED REPRINT OF A
HARDCOVER EDITION PUBLISHED BY HODDER & STOUGHTON. FOR INFORMATION ADDRESS
HODDER & STOUGHTON, 338 EUSTON ROAD, LONDON NW1 3BH, ENGLAND

FIRST PLUME PRINTING, FEBRUARY 2005   10 9 8 7 6 5 4

CIP DATA IS AVAILABLE. ISBN 0-452-28623-9
PRINTED IN THE UNITED STATES OF AMERICA

BOOKS ARE AVAILABLE AT QUANTITY DISCOUNTS WHEN USED TO PROMOTE PRODUCTS OR SERVICES. FOR INFORMATION PLEASE WRITE TO PREMIUM MARKETING
DIVISION, PENGUIN GROUP (USA) INC., 375 HUDSON STREET, NEW YORK, NEW YORK 10014.

WITH THANKS TO

KEVIN CECIL, ARTHUR MATHEWS, POLLY FABER,
CAMILLA HORNBY, TRENA KEATING AND ALL AT
PLUME, FREYA AYRES, DAVID AYRES.

3 BALLS
£1

EPILOGUE